PASSION BLUES

by Ramona Cecille Daily

In memory of

ALICE MAY HARRIS MCCONNEY

100,000 THANKS

Thanks to Leigh Feather, I appreciate all you did to help me with this book from formatting to drawing to giving me good orderly direction. The inspiration for the cover art came from Ramona Simone Carroll, my oldest grown daughter. When she was 5 she came home from Vacation Bible School with a stick figure of the cross with a heart in the center. I'll never forget she explained, "Jesus died on the cross and left us his heart." Thank you, Mona.

I also thank Amazon for printing my writings. A dream that was deferred and now realized!

HALLELUJAH!

THE FLOW

BAPTIZED CHILD OF GOD

Baptized child of God
Baptized child of God
Dead
Burried
Rising up as a
Baptized child of God
Baptized child of God
Living
Forgiving
Gushing out as a
Baptized child of God
Baptized child of God
SPLASH!

THE LORD IS...

The Lord is my Mother,
I want for nothing.
She lays me down at night.
She takes my hand by day
as we stroll by the sea.
She makes me feel good about myself.
She guides me
in the right direction
for Her Name's sake.
Sometimes I must walk through lonely alleys,
but You're with me Mom.
Your wit and your compassion,
they encourage me.
You prepare me a strengthening meal
in front of those who would make fun of me.
You bathe me in Your perfumed oil,
Your love spills over me.
I expect good and even greater things
to happen to me.
And I will be at home
in the Lord's house forever.

GOOD MORNING JESUS

Good morning Jesus
You're here with all your might.
Good morning Jesus.
You prayed us through the night.
We're getting use to You
Living within.
Good morning Jesus.
We're kin.

You're in us right now
We praise you "Oh Wow"
You won't leave us alone.
Casting out our blues
giving us True News.

Good morning Jesus
here we are again
Good morning Jesus
You're our true best Friend
We're getting use to You
Living within
Good morning Jesus
We're kin.

ABIDE
(to the tune of "Abide With Me")

Abide in me, I am the living vine
If you abide your life will be
divine.
Fear and despair in all this world
you see.
Your only hope is to abide
in me.

No money now, no money
coming in
Don't let this ever lead you
down to sin.
I am your Helper I have made
you free.
I do not change at all
abide in me.

Doctor does not know what is giving
Pain
there is no label,
thinks you are
insane.
I am your Doctor,
Holy Trinity,
whether you're sick or well
abide in me.

Death has crept in and yanked
your love away.
Do not know what to do
but you do not
stray.
Stay close my child
I am the victory
In life in death
O still abide in me.

PASSION BLUES

Refrain:
Pain in the morning,
Pain in the afternoon.
I got pain this morning,
I got pain this afternoon.
I can't get no comfort,
I'm gonna leave here soon,

Right now I feel,
feel like a fatherless chile.
I feel right now,
just like a fatherless chile.
When you turn your back on me,
Lord! I can't see you smile.

Refrain

The nails in my body
slowly breaking me.
The sin on my body
surely killing me.
I'm poured out like water
All I know is misery.

Refrain

This heart of mine
it won't pump no more
I said, This heart of mine
it won't pump no more
I'm gonna quit breathing
pass on to the other shore.

Refrain

EASTER

Burn those death rags
dress in glad rags
Dance pure joy
in poly-rythym
resurrection

AUNT ANNIE

Auntie died in bed
amidst pansies, petunias, porchulaca
died in the
soil of her toil.
Family shocked
as if death
were a myth.
Oh no! O yes!
Auntie died in
her beloved flower bed
just so.
I too would like to die planted in love.

FAITHFUL TREES

Barren winter trees
stand tall
as if Summer filled their arms
with flowers, leaves and fruit
teaching faithfulness
to a people
bereft of hope

THE MAN I LOVE

He treats me
sweet and gentle
the way he should
but he's got it bad
so its no good
He loves me
not himself
He cares for me
and hurts himself
but I love him
and each time he
punctures himself
I cry out in pain
yet he's relieved
happy its over
...only begun
I have 2 lovers
some times I feel
shame
for the one who
knows not
he's beloved
I give up
I let go
You love him
into loving himself...Please!
He takes up 58%
of my mind
time after time
so I worry about me
who am I?
& why do I
knit myself to his problems?
When I've got
plenty of my own
emptiness
forsaken-ess
illness

As I write this
I feel, I feel
love with freedom
taking a stand
I am who I am
Beloved
Writer, Dancer, Jokester
Mamma, Nanny, Daughter/Sister
Beloved
Lover of him
I am who God
says I am.

Habakkuk 3:17 – 19

HABAKKUK

Though I get paralyzed
and the docs don't know why
Though my husband is depressed
and having side-effect tremors
Though I sneeze my head off
and my nose continually drips
Though I am anxious
and cannot sleep 8 hours
Though I feel listless
and I isolate myself
Though I can't always remember
and have difficulty concentrating
Though my health insurance ends soon
and my disability is shaky
Yet I will still trust God until I die
God has stayed with me through it all
God is always the way for me
Hallelujah! Anyhow!

THERE IS POWER IN THE CROSS

Would we be free from boasting and pride?
There is pow'r in the cross, pow'r in the cross.
Open our hearts up to God's Crucified;
There is glorious pow'r in the cross.

Refrain:
There is pow'r, pow'r life producing pow'r
In the cross of the Lord.
There is pow'r, pow'r life producing pow'r
In the rugged cross of the Lord.

Would we give up our old childish ways?
There's pow'r, pow'r in the cross.
And let tough love of Christ rule our days;
There is glorious pow'r in the cross.

Refrain

Would we be willing to use all our gifts?
There is pow'r, pow'r in the cross.
Giving our neighbors the Spirit's lift;
There is glorious pow'r in the cross.

Refrain

Would we thank Jesus for all he has done?
There's pow'r in the cross, power in the cross.
Look to the cross and see victory won.
There's glorious power in the cross.

Refrain

THIRSTY FOR JESUS

Thirsty for Jesus
she came to the cross
poured out her whiskey
her tastebuds had lost
the desire.

Filled with living water
she now came alive,
pouring out to others
who desired to be revived
by Jesus.

TO KNOW GOD

To know, know God
is to Love, Love, Love God.
Just to see God's smile
Makes our lives worthwhile.
To know, know God
is to Love, Love, Love God.
Help us to. We want to. Yes, we do.

To Love, Love, Love God
is to serve, serve, serve God.
Just to see God's smile
Makes our life worthwhile.
To Love, Love, Love God
is to serve, serve, serve God.
Help us to. We want to. Yes, we do.

YOUNG BLACK MEN ("AMEN")

Refrain:
Young Black men, Young Black men,
Save our young Black men, Black men!

Trayvon Martin, the child in Ferguson,
"I Can't breathe..."
Save our young Black men, Black men!

Refrain

Most are unknown, only to their families,
Only to their communities
Save our young Black men, Black men!

Refrain

They're no longer with us,
They're blood cries out to us...
Save our young Black men, Black men

Refrain

Father, you created them,
Spirit, sustain them
Save our young Black men, Black men

Refrain

WALKING ON MY KNEES

Walking on my knees
asking "Please"
for the ones I birthed
and the ones they birthed
the original family
for those I love
those who don't love me
for those I don't like
those who don't look like me
yet resemble You
usurp my will:
let sorrow weep
over joy
joy leap
over sorrow—
"Thank You"

Judges 4.17 – 22

JAEL, WOMAN WARRIOR

Look at the arm muscles
on that woman.
With hammer in one hand and
and stake in the other
she pitches her family's tent
where her husband directs,
away from their people
away from their God.
Perhaps she prays,
Yaweh, forgive our falling away.

With hammer in one hand
and stake in the other
she performs her assigned task
as God directs,
driving the stake through the enemy's head.
Jael, driven by obedience to God.

ENOUGH!

You don't have enough. You don't do enough. You are not enough! These messages get conveyed through the media in the US and are echoed in the ways we are often treated in our society by one another. In other words you are a nobody unless you have/do/are this, this and this. The list keeps changing so no one can keep up to the implied expectations.

More is the idol that demands our love, obedience, our devotion and time. How much time do we think about getting more? Albert Einstein has written for our edification: "Any intelligent fool can make things bigger, more complex, and more violent. It takes a touch of genius— and a lot of courage—to move in the opposite direction". (Source unknown) The opposite direction is downward not upward mobility.

I have a friend who has been living in downward mobility for most of her life. She was a nurse who felt called to be a writer. She went back to school to develop her gift of writing. After graduating with a monetary writing award from Temple University she felt another call to go to California. Screenplays were her forte. She wanted to write movies that would inspire.

Jean was divorced. Her husband had PTSD from the Vietnam war. She has two children. Her son is speech delayed and her daughter did not have any medical problems. They lived in a house where the land in the neighborhood was sinking. She baked and sold cheesecakes to save up money for their trip to California from Philadelphia.

Many of her friends went to the Greyhound bus station to send them off. Yes, Jean and her children took the bus to California. A woman who was a member of her uncle's church in California opened her home to Jean and her children. Jean took on the job of a journalist for a small town newspaper. This stunted her creative energy.

She started a Teen Theater where young high school students could learn how to act and write. She founded a writer's club for struggling writers like herself. Jean is an encourager. Her children flourished. Her faith bloomed.

The woman with whom she lived took in her estranged husband who was terminally ill. Jean and her children moved into his house. Her writing turned to poetry and she published a few volumes. She does performance poetry that is prophetic in the sense of truth telling. She has not made the "big screen" or the "big time". Yet she has touched young and old with her words that come from the heart. Her children, friends and community rise up and call her blessed.

Not Have Enough

A woman told her sister, I want Christmas to be opulent! Rich in a wealthy way. We are programmed by society to acquire more and more to feel good about ourselves. But how long does that last, for real? The truth is that most of us have too much stuff. If we were in the crowd that Jesus fed by a miracle some of us would pull out five types of fish in large quantities. But would we want to share? Hording is an issue in our culture. We have a fear of scarcity. Unlike the Christians in South Africa who welcome the US visitors by splurging on us out of their poverty.

Not Do Enough

A man works from sun to sun but a woman's work is never done. Is that old adage still true today with all the gender freedoms that our mothers and grandmothers did not experience? Whether man or woman many of us feel we do not do enough even though there is no time to do more. There can be unrealistic demands from without and within. We can be oppressed by them. Where is the sabbath, rest, in our lives?

Not Enough

When we do not measure up to these unrealistic demands we may feel like we are not enough. We feel empty and less than others. Low self esteem runs rampant in the US. It spills over to all our relationships. It is contagious. Where is God in all of this?

A wise woman from Bible study once asked, "What is enough?" The question hung in the air like the question Pilate asked Jesus, "What is truth?" (John 18:38) Each of us needs to figure out how many shoes, gadgets and meals we need. The important word is need. "And my God will satisfy every need of yours according to his riches in in glory in Christ Jesus." (Philippians 4:19)

The media and popular culture creates the illusion that our wants are our needs. Living in the Land of Opportunity we get bamboozled into believing that having our wants met is an inalienable right. Having clarity to distinguish needs from wants requires a discerning heart and mind.

The One who is More than Enough sees us in a different way than US culture. This One had it all and gave it all up for us. Downward mobility. Jesus has made us enough. A 12-Step spirituality affirmation states: I HAVE ENOUGH. I DO ENOUGH. I AM ENOUGH.

Genesis 2.7

GOD'S BREATH

Sometimes our lives take our breath away. Not that they are breath-taking moments but tedious times when we are too busy in our heads and/or calendars. We worry about anything and everything that never comes to be. We are too preoccupied to be peaceful, thoughtful or mindful.

Too bad. We miss the forsythia, the sunset, and the incremental beauty of children growing up in front of our frenzied selves. We want to be peaceful, thoughtful or mindful but we are afraid that we will not "make it" in the world. Achieve what we have set out to achieve. That we will be stuck behind the "8 ball", whatever that means to us. That we, too, will lose our job, our house, our health, our health insurance, our loved one and live on the streets; which seems to be a trend in the USA. So we stay up nights worrying. We work harder to gain the illusion of job security and forget we did not give the breath of life to ourselves.

What else can we do? Remember reality? We are creatures, not Creator. We are creative and not workaholics. There is another way. A way out of the fray. A way into peaceful, thoughtful, mindful lives. But how or Who? God makes a way for us everyday. For the God of Abraham and Sarah; Mary, Joseph and Jesus still gives us breath. Not our boss, not our family or even ourselves. God, through the Spirit of Jesus, gives us eternal breath one day at a time. You may have forgotten this or never knew this reality. That does not make it less true. God gives us God's breath all the time.

God is intimately close to our breathing. When we fear the world we can breathe out fear and inhale faith in God's faithfulness never to leave us to breathe on our own. Breathe out fear. Breathe in faith in God. When we breathe God's breath life is not so scary. Life begins and ends with God's breath.

James 2.13

MERCY

I often say, "Lord, have mercy",
when confronted with something
outstandingly bad or good. It is one of
the oldest prayers of the Christian Way.
It is the root of the Jesus prayer: "Lord
Jesus Christ, Son of God, have mercy
on me a sinner." This prayer reminds
me who Jesus is and who I am in
relationship to the Father of all mercies.
But do I offer mercy to others when
they have offended me? They need
mercy from God that comes through
me. God, you want me to show my
enemies what mercy is. But I am so
busy judging my enemies or myself
that there is no room in my heart for
your mercy. I want to protect my hurt
feelings, my righteous indignation, my
desire for revenge. But you do not treat
me like that. Over and once again you
show me your sweet face of mercy.
Teach me how to show mercy when I
want to bare my teeth. Help me to let
mercy triumph over my judgmental
attitude. I hear you saying to me,
"Mona, have mercy!" Amen

FORGIVENESS

Forgiveness is a beautiful and an illusive gift. Most of us want to be forgiven for something that we did that we cannot make right. We feel badly, not just because we were caught acting ugly. We ache with remorse for our thoughts and actions that do not jibe with our sensibilities. The thought of making amends embarrasses and shames us. Often we hesitate to ask for forgiveness of our neighbor and of God. We think they will withhold this precious gift from us.

When someone hurts us by stepping on our toes accidentally forgiveness may roll off of our lips automatically. We may think ill of them and live silently with the pain. When a loved one hurts us over and over again intentionally or by accident how can we forgive? No one deserves to be hurt and wounded by anyone else, especially a loved one. Wanting to forgive that person prematurely may be unhealthy for the relationship.

Forgiveness absorbs pain whether it is physical, emotional or spiritual. Jesus forgave from the cross before we even asked to be forgiven. He took on the weight of initiating forgiveness for us, who accidentally and intentionally hurt God, our neighbor and ourselves. Jesus absorbed the pain that allows forgiveness to come up from the heart of God to the lips of Jesus. "Father forgive them for they know not what they do."

We are not God so it is very difficult to forgive. However the Spirit of Jesus lives in us and can change our hearts. When we offer forgiveness from the heart we are imitating God. Actually God is forgiving the person, institution, nation, religion through us. Forgiveness is a beautiful gift. Once received forgiveness can be given away.

Job 1.21

VULNERABLE

"But I don't want to be naked," said my then 5 year-old-son. He did
not want to wear his short sleeve summer shirt. It made him feel naked,
vulnerable. I did not understand. He was teaching me that each of us
feels vulnerable for different reasons. I do not want to be naked either.
When all hell breaks loose in our lives we can feel naked/vulnerable. Job
lost, children, livelihood, house loss, and the loss of of his wife's faith in
God. Grief and loss may leave us feeling unprotected from the changes
of life.

Job knew how this felt. He experienced one trauma piled upon another
in one day. He was in economic ruin and personal grief for his seven
children's deaths. Maybe you have your own traumas that you are trying
to live through. Job is an example in the Bible of a person who when
everything in his life went wrong he saw through God's eyes. Job knew
everything he had, possessions and children, were a gift from God.
He believed if God chose to take these from him he would not stop
trusting God. Job knew God to be trustworthy. Not because he was
rich in material things and blessed with many children. But because Job
spent time with God in worship and prayer. Job knew God and new
himself to be naked/vulnerable even before this catastrophe happened
to him. And it was OK with him. Job learned to bless God anyhow!

Job 1.21b

PATIENCE

The patience of Job. Patience has to do with acceptance of the way things are not in defeat but in reality. Most things we cannot change. Yet we spend much of our time and energy trying to change our situation or the other person. We are impatient for God to act on our behalf. We doubt God will be with us as promised. That God cares about our feeble lives when we are sick, poor, in danger. If we were in Job's mess, many of us would put up our hands, curse God and die.

Instead Job does an amazing thing. He blesses God's authority over his life situations. Job received abundant blessings from God. Now they were all gone for no obvious reason. His faith was not in prosperity, upward mobility or even his good relationship with God. Job's faith was in God who is in charge. In this verse Job is patient with God's sovereignty. He believes God can do what God wants when God wants with whoever.

We live in an impatient society. We think we earned the right to have things instantly because we are so smart, just look at our phones. Waiting is discouraged especially waiting for God to do something. It is easier to blame God or our neighbor for the ills in our lives. Because that is a quick and simplistic solution.

We do not know what God is up to. God is not telling right now. Therefore we are impatient and angry. Angry that our fortunes have changed. But we do not use our anger constructively. We do not have a little talk with God about it. We try to manipulate our situation to have the best outcome. We do not give God elbow room to use God's elbow grease in our lives. Then we miss out on an eyeball to eyeball encounter with the living God which can deepen our relationship. We miss an opportunity to learn how to truly say, "I will bless the Lord at all times". (Psalm 34.1)

John 11.38 – 44

LIVING DEAD

Lazarus was probably satisfied and comfortable. His sickness was healed through death. He was fine sleeping in Sheol waiting for the last day. Laz was done with the trouble of this world. Or so he thought.

Then here comes his dear friend, boon coon buddy, Jesus, late and wrong, to disturb his slumber. Shaking up his accepted death, his quietude with a command to come back in the fray of life. His sisters' anger with and blaming of Jesus for letting Laz die cannot be compared with what Laz may have felt by making him live. Annoyed, angry, displaced, happy, sad, excited, amazed, confused...He could have blamed Jesus for calling him back to life, having to die again, back into the trouble of this world. In this world you do have trouble.

Everyone rejoiced when Laz hopped out of the cave all bound up but alive. After being loosed did he walk around like the living dead, a zombie, constricted in body, baffled in time and space, unable to articulate his feelings. The text is mute on Laz's response to Jesus calling him forth. Plenty room for the imagination of another to run wild.

Has Jesus ever done that to you? Betrayed you by dragging you back to the scene of your suffering after rescuing you from it. Did Jesus ever disturb your peaceful solitude with the praises of others. People who are vocal when you want to be in a dream-like state of nirvana?

Jesus comes with a sword as well as with a cup of cold water. He carries a whip and a warm blanket. Jesus is our Precious Friend but sometimes He feels like an enemy. He brings us out of our boundary of comfort to do the uncomfortable, to live, to obey, to answer His call to come forth when we are safely wrapped up and hidden away.

How is Jesus calling you out of your comfortable cave/tomb today? Laz was obedient even though he may have felt gypped. Will you, like Lazarus, obey Him anyway?

Matthew 25.31 – 46

SORTING OUT

Sisters from the Deaconess Community* are sent out to serve love to the neighbor as if the neighbor was Jesus. Our neighbors are from every nation. They may not believe like us or look like us but they are created in the image of God.

This sorting out that Jesus does in Matthew is not between nations like we do in this world. It is separating those who see Jesus in those in need and help to meet their need. They do it for Jesus' sake. Not to be recognized for their good works. They desire to do what God has called them to do: feed the hungry, help stop malaria, provide clean drinking water, welcome the stranger, clothe the naked, visit the sick at home and in the hospital, visit those who are in the prison system, protest the against violence, welcome the newly released, change the system of oppression. Am I a good sheep today?

*Women consecrated for Word and Service in The Evangelical Lutheran Church in America and in the Evangelical Lutheran Church in Canada.

STREAMING JESUS
a chancel drama

SCENE 1
(Older woman is watching her soaps. She is talking to the TV characters. Then she sees Jesus on to the TV screen. She gets down on her knees and says:)

My Lord and my God!

SCENE 2
(Jogger is in motion listening to iPod. Hears "I am the Alpha and Omega." The jogger says, Who? looks up gets on knees saying:)

My Lord and my God!

SCENE 3
(A person showing a power point of what the church did last year. Looks at the screen with his lazer pointer. Person gasps as he falls on his knees:)

My Lord and My God!

SCENE 4
(Children playing "X box" suddenly say:)

"That looks like Jesus on the X box. Let's pray": (They get on their knees and put their palms together and bow their heads together facing each other.)

SCENE 5
(Family of 4 watching 4 different devices for watching movies. They say together, but not in unison:)

Do you see what I see? (On their knees where they are, they say:)

My Lord and my God!

SCENE 6
Pastor comes up and asks:
Where have you seen Jesus this week?

NOBODY KNOWS

Refrain:
Nobody knows the rage I feel,
Nobody knows but Jesus.
Nobody knows the rage I feel,
Glory Hallelujah!

Sometimes I'm hot, sometimes I'm cold.
Oh, yes God.
Sometimes I feel I will explode.
Oh, yes God.

Refrain

Though I seem to wear a smile.
Oh, yes God.
My bowels are filled up with guile.
Oh, yes God.

Refrain

Will this rage consume me? No!
Oh, yes God.
God teach me how to let it go...
Oh, yes God.

Refrain

ANGER

Rationally release
anger
before sundown
or
ugliness will set in
before dawn.

THE DANCE OF DEATH

Death keeps wooing me:
Your heart could give out.
Death whispers:
Breast cancer could be
your undoing.
Death teases:
You could die
while paralyzed.
Death courts me with sour notes.
Nothing has worked
yet
I will dance
cheek-to-cheek
with death
a moment
Spending the rest of Life
Partying in the Lamb's
Marriage Feast.

OUR GOD

Our God is fluent in sheer silence
practice this language
with our GOD

NODDING YOUR HEART

The hand pierced High Priest
bends way down
receiving repairing.
Only God can take you to the
eternal realm.
A spaced out soul,
nodding but not agreeing
is high in the depths
of oblivion.
But the hand pierced High Priest
bends way down
receiving repairing.
Only God can take you to the
eternal realm.
Just nod your heart in agreement.
Agree by nodding
your heart.

Made in the USA
San Bernardino, CA
05 January 2017